The 10 Commandments of Client Appreciation

Thou Shalt Create Loyalty

A Step-by-Step Guide to No. 1 Position

1st edition

Darrell Hardidge

Disclaimer

The material in this manuscript is not to be distributed or copied in any way without the written permission of the author. The 10 Commandments of Client Appreciation and all diagrams in the manuscript are the property of Darrell Hardidge. All the information, techniques, skills and concepts contained within this publication are of the nature of general comment only and are not in any way recommended as individual advice. The intent is to offer a variety of information to provide a wider range of choices now and in the future, recognising that we all have widely diverse circumstances and viewpoints. Should any reader choose to make use of the information contained herein, this is their decision, and the contributors (and their companies), authors and publishers do not assume any responsibilities whatsoever under any condition or circumstances. It is recommended that the reader obtain their own independent advice.

First Edition 2017 Copyright © Darrell Hardidge 2017

Creator: Darrell Hardidge, author.

The 10 Commandments of Client Appreciation – Thou Shalt Create Loyalty – A Step-by-Step Guide to No. 1 Position / Darrell Hardidge.

1st edition

ISBN 10: 1981442022 (paperback)
ISBN 13: 9781981442027 (paperback)

Sales management.

Customer relations

Relationship marketing.

Published by Saguity

www.Saguity.com

For further information about orders:

contact@saguity.com

Dedication

There are those who step up to be counted. These are the leaders; they take risks while others stand on the sidelines. Observers play it safe while leaders move forward where no path exists. Leaders understand that client appreciation is the future; they discard client satisfaction. Why? Satisfied clients are prone to defect; appreciative clients have a higher probability of remaining loyal.

This book is dedicated to the great leaders. Those who believe in going beyond the competition and making a stand for their reputation and commitment by showing the way. Never lose sight or belief that going the extra mile isn't worth the journey, it always is.

Trust in your values and intuition. Being of service to your clients will always be appreciated and rewarded.

Acknowledgements

To my awesome team at Saguity. I am continually amazed at how we keep getting better. Your belief in our mission and values to educate the world on the benefits of mastering client appreciation is what drives our innovation and discovery. I am so grateful for your commitment.

To our clients who place enormous trust in our integrity. We will never stop finding ways to innovate and implement your market-leading edge.

To the special few who have been so generous with your time and patience. Your commitment and support with reviewing the manuscript is greatly appreciated.

To Michael Stillwell and Steve Psaradellis, thanks again for being such a positive disturbance with this manuscript. Your insight and ideas are always so valuable and powerful.

To Sue, thank you for being my greatest support and for your extraordinary patience and belief in this new discovery. Together we are better.

Table of Contents

Foreword

Today, business leaders are faced with fast-changing markets, ever-tightening budgets, and customers who demand ever-increasing levels of satisfaction. Given these challenges, where do manufacturers, retailers and professional service providers turn for effective measurement, helpful insights and wisdom?

In our monthly CEO Institute syndicate meetings, members constantly grapple with issues and topics focusing on people management, systems, processes and business structures accompanied by regular discussions around the challenge of effective and productive business development strategies and tactics. Once again, the question is 'Where do we turn to for insights?'

Like Moses descending from Mount Sinai with two carved stone tablets providing guidance to the masses on how to live better lives, perhaps we can look to Darrell's book for insights on how to effectively measure and understand Client Appreciation. It enables us to understand how to create a real and enduring sense of loyalty amongst our clients to build strong and lasting repeat and referral bases, and to develop step-by-step strategies to drive our businesses to the number one positions in our chosen markets.

From our perspective as business owners, Darrell's methodology provided our family business with greater insights into the client experience journey — how each of the touchpoints throughout that journey contribute to the overall client experience, level of satisfaction and appreciation. We gained an understanding of what we do that keeps clients coming back and referring friends and colleagues to us for their vehicle purchases and servicing requirements. It also gave us insights into the where and how we sometimes get it horribly wrong, and the damaging consequences that such actions inevitably generate.

For larger businesses, especially those operating from multiple sites and locations, Darrell provides a methodology and insights into how we might utilise client research and responses to understand our outliers, our high-performing achievers who demonstrate consistent levels of client experience and retention. You don't need to be told that extreme client loyalty of this magnitude drives consistently high levels of sales performance and business profitability. Knowing who our outliers are and the behaviours that they demonstrate provides a benchmark to lift the balance of our business up to. That has certainly been our experience and is mirrored through Darrell's research and experience with Saguity's long-term and appreciative clients.

I commend Darrell's book to you. The approach articulated will challenge traditional concepts and thinking around client appreciation measures and methodologies. However, the proof is in the outcomes — our business, like many of Saguity's clients, has improved from the experience.

Michael Stillwell

Chairman Stillwell Motor Group, CEO Institute Syndicate Chairman

Chapter 1
Introduction

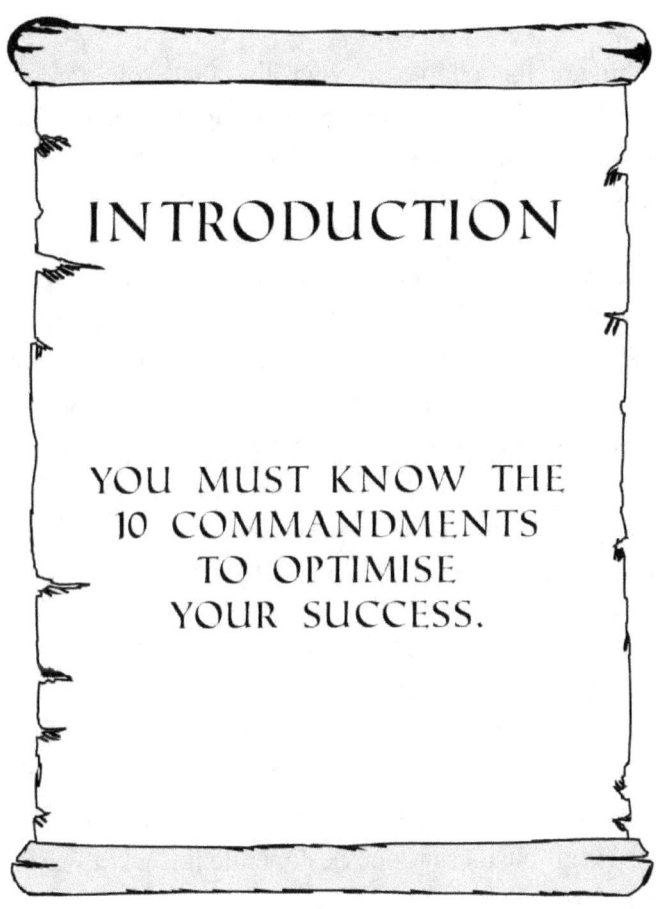

Who are the people in your life you truly appreciate? How important are they to you? Consider the significance they have been in some of your critical decisions.

Who are the people in your life that you are just satisfied with? Are these people significant in your day-to-day success? How do they differ to the ones you truly appreciate?

The people we appreciate are highly relevant to us. Their existence makes our life better, more meaningful and we have a heart connection to them. The people we are just satisfied with are not so significant. They haven't done anything wrong; it's just more of a head connection. They're not a vital part of our day to day activities; if you didn't see them for a while, it wouldn't bother you.

Business is the same. We deal with businesses we appreciate and businesses we are satisfied with. The 10 Commandments of Client Appreciation are about understanding the emotional connection businesses have to their market. It's also a 'how to' book to ensure all business processes operate in such a way to guarantee client appreciation.

Chapter 1: Introduction

You are holding the proven methods of mastering client appreciation as practised by leading companies and rated by their market. This book is the bible of client experience appreciation. With over half a million real-time client experience interviews conducted by my company, Saguity, we thought it was time to share the results with a wider audience.

While many businesses strive for satisfaction, those reaching for appreciation are experiencing extreme client loyalty, client referrals and repeat spending. It isn't luck or the economy to credit for leading businesses being where they are. It is carefully engineered processes covering all parts of the operation that are geared towards achieving client appreciation. The 10 Commandments of Client Appreciation are for every business and are the foundations for fostering an appreciative client base.

Upon hearing I was planning to share these commandments publicly, there was some concern within my circle. Some people in my own life said, 'Why would you do that? Why not keep it for your clients exclusively to have a point of difference.'

I was surprised by this reaction at first, but they were forgetting the one critical factor that's not present in this book.

There's a distinction that's missing here that we can't help you with; you either have it or you don't. It can't be taught, yet all leading businesses have it.

The distinction is: Your drive and desire to enhance yourself and your business in every respect to operate at an optimal level to be No.1.

The path to market dominance is never made by those who accept the status quo or who are content with 'satisfied'. Only those with drive and desire even attempt it. With the commandments in this handbook, the path is clear; it's in a series of foundations that you are holding in your hand *right now*.

How do we know this works? The results speak for themselves; our clients are leading in their respective industries. We discovered a predictable pattern that, when followed, will produce profound results in a company's bottom line. The size or form of your business doesn't matter — single location, franchise, dealership, multiple site, large sales team or small. This book is highly relevant to every company.

Essentially, by following a very precise and strategic protocol, we have a process of understanding WHY clients act the way they do in regard to their loyalty.

Chapter 1: Introduction

We have the privilege of interviewing on behalf of the best businesses in Australia — companies that have defined themselves on *who they are* rather than *what they do*.

From our research, we know these great businesses implement a combination of business distinctions (The 10 Commandments of Client Appreciation). They are consistently being innovated and reviewed. This pursuit of optimising client experience is what keeps them No.1.

Unless you innovate and work on connecting with your market, *you'll suffer during the shift in client experience disruption that's occurring now*. There is more change happening in the way you can connect with your market than ever before. The few points of difference left to any business are in *their client experience process*.

Leading companies know this and are acting differently. They are asking better questions and using experts to help them understand and design their client experience process. They invest in high-quality research and powerful analytics to help them better understand their market. They do not use generic online survey tools that blast their clients with spam emails and annoying SMSs. They understand the importance of mastering client experience and the critical role CX plays in their business.

They understand the need to uniquely define their market relevance and how to optimise their heart connection to their market. They measure their success by client appreciation.

If you believe engagement with your market is critical to your success and you wish to operate above your competitors and enjoy the fruits of client relevance and extreme loyalty, congratulations — you now have the bible to get there, and we look forward to supporting you on your journey to greatness.

Different isn't always better, but better is always different. The 10 Commandments of Client Appreciation teach you how to be both better and different.

Chapter 2
Commandment I
WHY

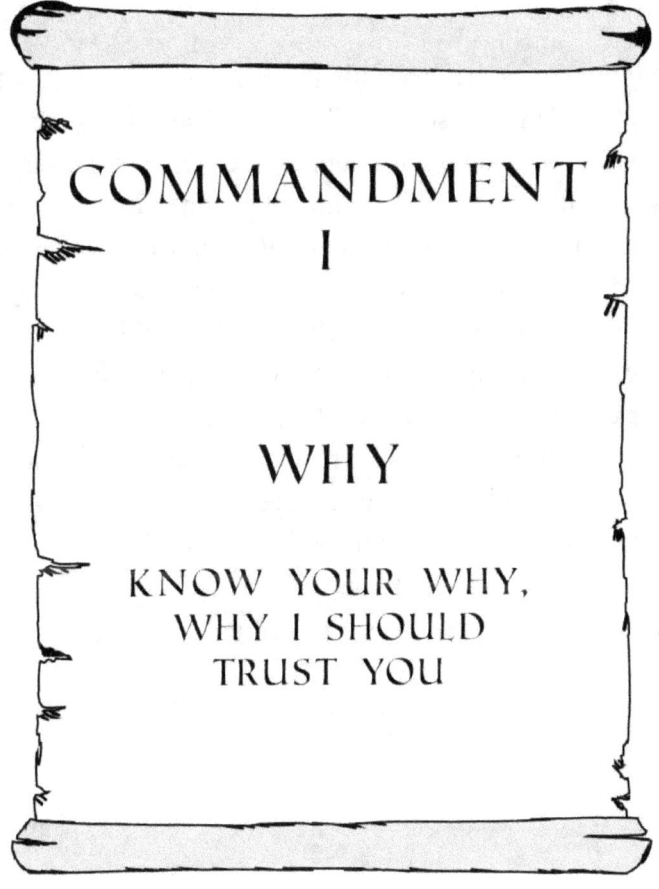

COMMANDMENT
I

WHY

KNOW YOUR WHY,
WHY I SHOULD
TRUST YOU

Kids are great at asking 'WHY?' The same question can be asked of your company. WHY should I do business with you? WHY are you so special? WHY should I trust you? WHY should I give you my extreme loyalty? All very valid and important questions.

Simon Sinek has a brilliant TED Talk called 'Start with WHY'. I show this in workshops wherever possible (go to youtube.com and search 'Simon Sinek start with why', the 18-minute version). It challenges team members to think about their purpose and role in a company. If their purpose is only for the pay, then it's all about themselves and there is no way they are going to protect your client experience process and future client relationships. In fact, if their employment has no other purpose than the money, it's predicted you will at best achieve a service standard of client satisfaction. This leaves your business at risk of being left behind by your competitors and stuck in a price trap.

BEING OF
SERVICE HAS
THE EMPHASIS
ON BEING,
NOT
DOING.

People don't buy what you do, they buy WHY you do it. No.1 companies know they must connect with their market. They authentically express their desire to understand their clients' needs and wants. Being of service has the emphasis on **be**ing not **do**ing. If your team just follow the process of what to **do** and have no commitment to **be**ing their best for your clients, then client satisfaction will be your only reward and your potential downfall.

© Darrell Hardidge, Sagacity.com

Chapter 2: Commandment I - WHY

WHY must be at the heart of your company DNA. It must be the energy that drives purpose and commitment in everything you do.

Your leadership team must be the custodians of your WHY and protect it like their lives depend on it (because the life of your business does). They must be an example of the behaviour that creates extraordinary client experiences. They must lead the way beyond adversity and challenge. They must resist the temptation of *close enough is good enough*. As Dr John Demartini says, 'Until you have a purpose that's bigger than yourself you cannot expect to go beyond yourself.' 'Whatever it takes' is an action, not a theory, and the best companies have a 'true north' when it comes to their commitment to delivering amazing service experiences.

It's not about your record sales figures; it's about the joy you deliver to your market from showing how much you care. The impact and benefits of this commitment goes beyond the workplace and adds value to the personal lives of your team. Having the power of an authentic WHY (that isn't about the money) will provide your team with a deeper sense of purpose and inspire them to achieve greater things in their personal lives. This is what's known as the 'precession effect'.

Have you ever stayed in a hotel and been ripped off for Wi-Fi? It's a huge upsell; they make excellent margin but you feel cheated. The bean counters love it, but it's short sighted and impacts loyalty. There's good profit and bad profit. Good profit is achieved by adding value to your clients where they appreciate it and are happy to pay for it. Bad profit is when you leverage a situation and trap them into paying.

Our research confirms that when a company has a powerful WHY and a connected team, their clients express gratitude and appreciation for the efforts made to serve them. These companies are the real innovators of client experience (CX). Any change in the CX process must add optimal value to clients. If it increases profit but reduces service, it won't work. These are the quick fixes that are driven by a self-centred culture where it's only about the money and not the value. No.1 companies live by the rule that adding value is the most powerful way to engage your market and build an extremely loyal client base.

At Saguity, our WHY is to educate the world in the benefits of mastering client appreciation. By exceeding our clients' expectations we leave them appreciative and fulfilled. This is the epitome of a strong, viable and successful business — clients keep returning and become your best marketers by sharing their experiences with others.

Our research shows our clients their untapped opportunities in giving service excellence. In doing so they return to us to pursue their next level of service excellence to keep giving them the edge in their market. Our team know that every interview they do helps companies grow and protects the employment of their team. As a result, they protect themselves with exactly the same thing. We improve by a minimum of 1% per week by consistently reviewing what we do and asking how can we do it better.

What's your WHY? What drives your team to go beyond the standards of last week? What would happen if you had a culture truly committed to excellence and serviced your market with the highest standards of integrity?

Chapter 3
Commandment II
MASTER THE CX JOURNEY

COMMANDMENT
II

MASTER THE
CX JOURNEY

THOU SHALT KNOW
YOUR PATH

Think of the home you live in — if you've built a home, even better. A quality home is a perfect example of how client experience needs to be structured. A quality home cannot be built without planning and coordination. There is no point delivering the kitchen if the roof isn't on. Quality house construction is a finely tuned process where everyone knows their role and which part of the jigsaw they hold.

Your CX process needs to be constructed the same way. It must start with the planning and have a clearly defined outcome. A quality home requires a very high standard of workmanship and detail to be accepted by the owner. A quality CX process requires the same, with the outcome being a 10 out of 10 (10/10) client appreciation score. However, many companies have a client experience process that reflects the standard of a very dodgy tradesmen who works to the theory 'if we can get away with it...'

How often do you say as a frustrated consumer, 'Why don't they just do this. It's so simple?' Yet they don't, and you leave with an experience of 'it was OK', 'not too bad', 'average' or 'just satisfied'. We are left wondering why didn't they just try a little bit harder. It would have made a world of difference. It's

the small things that count, and very few companies
pay attention to these details.

A 10/10 client experience score ensures the basics are
covered (a minimum of what's expected), then going
the extra steps to create a point of difference.
Consider your own experiences of a great business.
It's often in the things that others overlook that leave
you feeling appreciated and valued. This is why you
become loyal to them.

A common term used today by CX managers is
'client centricity'. You may have heard, 'We are a
very client-centric company'. Whenever I hear this I
ask, 'Can you please explain how that works in a
simple description?' Often, I am left with a blank
look. Then they say, 'It's a part of our cultural values
and team engagement process' and 'It's designed to
ensure we place our clients at the centre of everything
we do'. I'm yet to have a simple explanation that
enables anyone to understand the basic principles of
client centricity.

EVERYTHING SPEAKS.

Chapter 3: Commandment II – MASTER THE CX JOURNEY

Let me explain what client centricity is in a very simple diagram. I use this in all my workshops and everyone gets it. Many times, people have said how our process enabled them to communicate the impact that every department has on their CX. Most importantly, the people who never thought they had a part to play in it now realise how critical their role is. I use a simple phrase that connects the team and creates a sense of balance: 'Everything Speaks'.

Everything you do in your business across all your departments and teams speaks volumes to your client base. I ensure the executive team especially get the fact that 'everyone' is responsible for client experience. No one is immune from the responsibility of creating a 10/10 service culture.

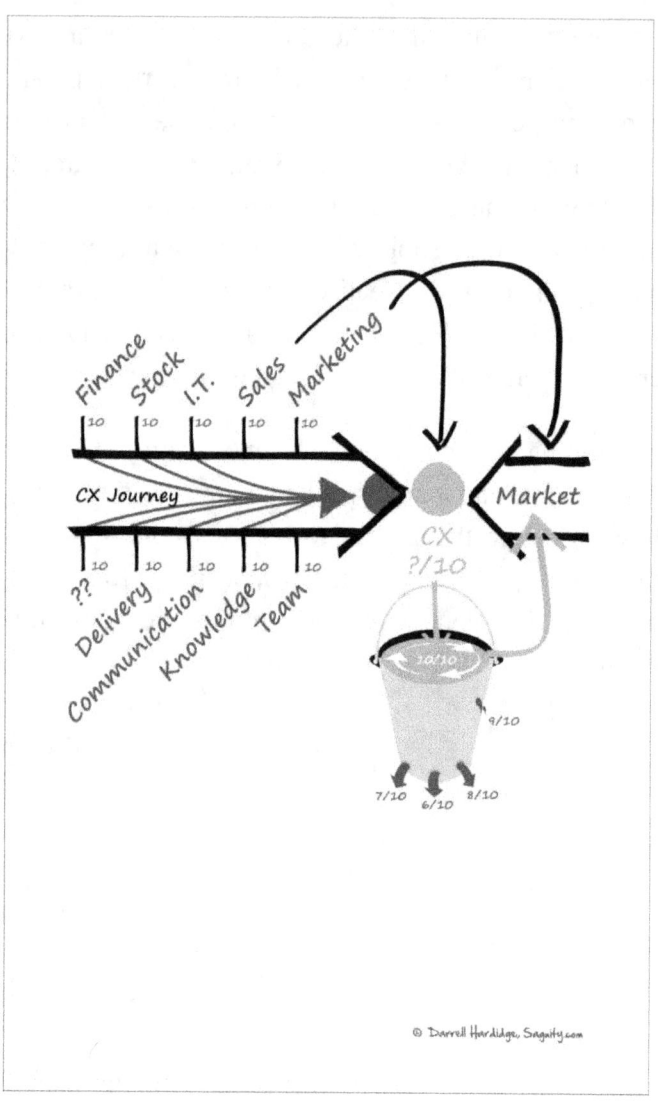

Chapter 3: Commandment II – MASTER THE CX JOURNEY

The arrow on the left side is you. The arrow on the right is your market. The touchpoints will vary from business to business. I have used the most common ones for this example in reference to a product or service that relies on repeat transactions. The objective is to identify how many touch points you have in your CX process. You will be surprised at how many touchpoints are not included in the current thinking around client centricity. The tip of the arrow reflects all the engagements with clients. We call this 'the sum of all experiences'.

Your Marketing Touchpoint (lead generation) has the objective to connect with carefully targeted and ideal prospects and to reconnect with your existing clients. Its purpose is to create attention, interest, desire, then action, and to engage with your sales process.

Your Sales Touchpoint (conversion) is critical for you to engage ideal clients. It will have many touch points within it to ensure a high-quality sales conversion process. The challenge with the sales touchpoint is it creates a very high degree of expectation on the delivery of your product or service. You will never hear a salesperson tell you their service is poor or their delivery is ordinary, or their help desk isn't helpful. We are always told that dealing with them is the right choice. Too often our consumer experiences are only average because we get treated as a transaction, with very little emotion or gratitude expressed. The sales process often sets up the client experience to fail and let the client down due to a poor structure of client centricity.

Your Team Touchpoint is multi-layered. In itself, it's another journey covering all departments and teams. The basics of this touchpoint must ensure, as a minimum, everyone clearly understands their role and its importance on CX. Remember, 'everything speaks' and if any area of your team dynamic is not client centric, it will let the business down.

Your Knowledge Touchpoint focuses on ensuring everyone has the training and experience they need to deliver the ideal 10/10 experience. New team members must have a mentor to support them to learn how to deliver excellence. Most companies assume that if a person has the skill for the task, they are ready to go. They are rarely tested on their ability to deliver excellence. No. 1 companies never assume; they review all areas of the business and their teams to ensure they have the right culture (see Commandment 5). If you don't ensure team knowledge is focused on 10/10, you could be importing the bad habits of the past. Your knowledge touchpoint must have the tip of the arrow always in its focus.

Your Finance Touchpoint

Nothing in business can kill a relationship faster than a dispute over money. If there are disputes, how effective are your team trained to professionally handle them? How well do they work with clients who make requests around payment? We have found the power of a close and respectful client relationship with the finance department makes a massive difference to overall CX. This is equally important around your process with suppliers. Make no mistake — if supply is short, the best relationships win every time on deciding who gets the product. A finance department that is difficult to deal with will often cause their company to have greater issues in the supply chain. Those who are a pleasure to deal with will always get preferential treatment. It's surprising how often a company loses revenue over supply issues when the real issue is their finance department's behaviour.

Your Delivery Touchpoint (product or service) is often the key human connection a business has to its market. With the focus on digital processes, the human connection is reducing rapidly. Smart companies know their team are their greatest asset and ensure their team clearly understand their responsibility to the client. Training your delivery team in service excellence is a wise investment because they reflect how the world experiences your company.

Your IT Touchpoint

Rule No.1 is 'Make it easy to buy from you'. It's amazing how difficult it can be to pay a company or to communicate with them. How well is your IT process connecting with your market? This is a never-ending challenge to master as technology is constantly changing. How often have you experienced a website that is difficult to use and wonder, 'Have they ever had to buy from themselves?' and 'Did anyone outside of the IT department test this process for its ease of use and client focus?' If you never ask clients for feedback, you may be losing a fortune because your system is too difficult. IT processes are a key frustration to the marketplace. Those who get it right win big time.

Zappos online were rewarded with becoming a billion-dollar shoe empire. They dominate a market by ensuring their IT is connected with their human process.

Your Supply Chain Touchpoint

Many companies are only as good as their supply chain. You can have the best intentions and processes, but if you can't deliver your product/service when requested, you could soon be out of business. Just as you want your clients to pay on time, be easy to deal with and give lifetime loyalty, your suppliers want exactly the same. You are their client, and your business is essential to them.

A big frustration that has evolved over the last few years is procurement. It wasn't long ago that it was a very rare thing to deal with. While procurement has many benefits, it has also been the cause of great client relationships failing. The focus on price, price, price and shopping around to play one against the other may look good on your balance sheet for a year or two — but wait and see how it evolves when this starts to impact your CX process and the tip of the arrow. The one thing your clients don't want to deal with is how your service has dropped because a decision was made to save a few bucks. Today's saving can be a massive loss tomorrow.

Your ?? Touchpoint

Talk with your team and determine what your next most critical touchpoint is. Consider how it impacts the tip of the arrow and your overall CX result. Most companies realise they have missed multiple channels and touchpoints across their business model when they design it with a 10/10 service experience in mind. Designing and implementing it takes time but it's money well invested. Anywhere you have a blind spot is potentially costing you a lot in how your market relates to your company.

The Matrix Effect

I have targeted a few key touchpoints in this example, each of which is a silo in the business model. However, it's critical to understand they all crisscross the business. This is why I say 'Everything Speaks'. No team member is immune to the impact they have on CX in your business. Everyone must ensure they understand everything from the supply chain to the market and how each part impacts CX.

Chapter 3: Commandment II – MASTER THE CX JOURNEY

The number one touchpoint end user clients say is the most frustrating is communication. This is by far the biggest complaint and most significant in impacting loyalty. It's vital you identify all the touchpoints in your business that have direct communication to your market and investigate the standards that are delivered. Usually it's the sales touchpoint that has the focus — however, your IT, finance, ordering, delivery, etc all must be designed with very high-quality communication.

Chapter 4
Commandment III
PLAN THE FIRST 15%

COMMANDMENT
III

PLAN THE
1ST 15%

THOU SHALT SLOW
DOWN TO SPEED UP

Planning the first 15% will cause great disturbance and despair for some. It will have you unpack so many parts of your business that some of you won't know where to start. For those who have their touchpoints well documented and honed, this will take your process to the next level.

The commandment of the first 15% was developed by Dr W Edwards Deming, the founder of the quality systems we use in everyday life like Six Sigma, Lean Manufacturing and the Just-In-Time (JIT) process. Dr Deming was the founder of the Japanese standard of quality. He developed the quality systems for Toyota, Cannon and Honda, to name a few. The highest business award you can win in Japan is the Deming Prize for excellence. Dr Deming is known as the ninth hidden turning point in world history. His innovations have impacted our day-to-day world to an extraordinary degree (search W Edwards Deming to learn about his impact on the world).

SLOW DOWN
TO
SPEED UP.

Chapter 4: Commandment III – PLAN THE FIRST 15%

This commandment is also known as 'the first 15% process'. From the many thousands of people I have presented to, this commandment hits hard for some and permanently changes the way they think about their business. The following diagram has two pathways to 100% completion. One has the first 85% in the red and the last 15% in the green; the other has the opposite. They both relate to exactly the same project. The defining difference is the approach to the planning and the thinking of optimal effectiveness within the first 15%. We see this a lot when we look at data where companies have multiple sites, dealerships or franchises to coordinate. This commandment defines the issues that many have around service standards and have not previously seen the problem. Get the first 15% right and the remaining 85% will follow the pattern. If you don't, then the first 85% will be full of waste and the last 15% will hopefully work.

The 1ˢᵗ 15%

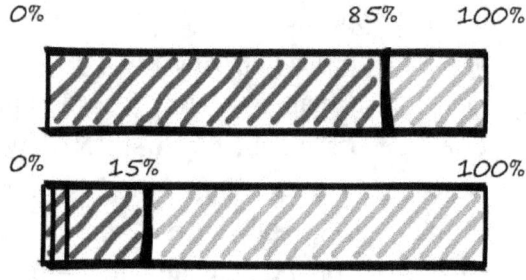

Must get the 1ˢᵗ 15% correct

**Slow Down
to
Speed Up**

© Darrell Hardidge, Saguity.com

Chapter 4: Commandment III – PLAN THE FIRST 15%

The easiest way to describe this process is to think about your own experiences. Think about a project that went really bad. It caused major stress, upset and a cost overrun. It's the one you wish had never happened. Yet the truth is, it was a defining moment and a great lesson for you (if you choose to see it that way).

Think back from the 100% point and unpack what happened. There will be significant errors that occurred along the way. Maybe at the 65% mark you realised you didn't have the resources you needed to deliver the timeline; or at the 40% mark you could see there was a budget blowout coming. At the 30% mark, the planning was wrong with suppliers, or at the 20% mark your team weren't briefed properly, etc. It's possible to unpack this project and determine where the errors were made. If you had to do it again, you would do it differently. Perhaps you realised you should never have done it in the first place as it was beyond your capabilities. This situation is often what sends companies broke.

Now think about your most successful project. The one often used to benchmark the ideal scenario. If you unpack this from 100% completion to the start, and as you mark the 80%-60%-40%-20% stages, you

Darrell Hardidge

will confirm it was all on track and well-coordinated with very tight communication. This may even reflect the skills of key people and suppliers who helped to create this result.

What really made it work? Discuss this with your team and you will find that by the 15% mark of the project, it was all coordinated and planned in detail. Everyone knew their responsibilities, suppliers were confirmed, clients were updated and educated. When things went off track they were quickly corrected; everyone was highly focused on their role and project updates were constant. Am I correct? This is what the first 15% is all about: getting the first 15% right will ensure the 85% follows easily. It is making sure your project is planned and time-lined.

Fifteen per cent still has a lot of waste, and No.1 companies know how to go two levels deeper. Apple don't make 100,000 iPhones and throw out 15,000 of them. Dr Deming had two further steps that defined this principle to a deeper level. The first 15% of the first 15%, which equals the first 2.25% of the project. This must be identified to ensure the 15% mark is totally predictable and on track. This breaks the project down even further to the structures that support the essential parts.

Chapter 4: Commandment III – PLAN THE FIRST 15%

Getting the first 15% right is like seeing this point at the 100% mark and then breaking it down again. This may sound complex but it's pretty simple if you get your team together and work on it. Make it visual on flip charts with post-it notes and map out all the steps. What would have to be done at the 15% mark to ensure the next 85% just works.

When you have this completed, start again at the initial 15% mark and work out what the steps would be to have all this sorted at 2.25%. You will be amazed at what you identify — all the simple things that when left out become big things later. These are always costly and ultimately impacting your CX process.

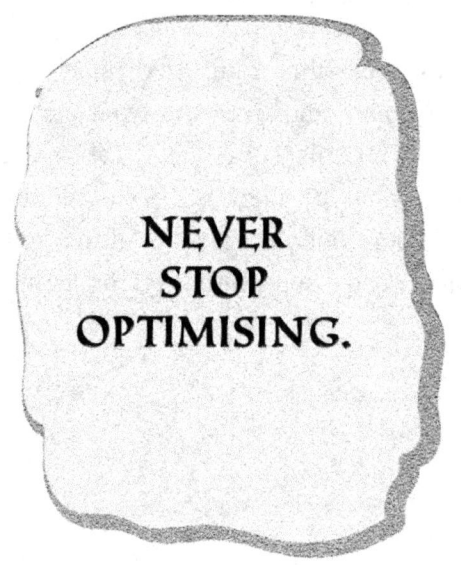

NEVER
STOP
OPTIMISING.

Chapter 4: Commandment III – PLAN THE FIRST 15%

There is another step in the Deming process where precision is achieved in major manufacturing operations. It's the first 15% of the first 15% of the first 15%, which equals the first 0.34% of the project. Seems hard to grasp. For example, this means 340 iPhones out of 100,000 would be discarded. This is where the highest levels of process operate. Aviation is an incredible example. There are literally thousands of flights daily, yet rarely is there a fault. Qantas Airlines apply this principle even tighter, they have the highest safety record and have never had a death from a crash. This proves the principle of checking and re-checking with the correct process. However, the first thing to master is the actual process and then manage it.

Where do you think one of the first areas a company will cut costs that impacts the first 15% in their business? Their Client Experience process. They cut labour and reduce costs of delivery, and take the human relationships out of their CX process. It doesn't show up for a while but when it does, it's like turning a big ship. Sometimes this poorly thought out strategy (usually made by people who just focus on number crunching) cannot be resolved as it's too late and many clients have left for good.

A key reason this goes unnoticed until it's too late is because the KPIs are incorrectly represented. Very few companies have the correct metric for measuring CX and client retention. Most use financials which reflect the history of the business and are not a measurement of client retention. It's like driving your business forward while only looking in your rear-view mirror. **You must have a metric that measures the future intentions of your clients. This way you get to test the impact of your current internal operations on CX.**

Saguity's 'Client Appreciation Index' (CAI™) produces a KPI that measures your current CX and scores it on a scale of 10/10. We measure repeat business, referrals, value for money, wallet share with competitors, your competitors' scores, your heart drivers (emotional connection), your head drivers (business processes), and how you manage significant requests, to name a few. Anywhere you score 0 to 8 out of 10, we go three levels deep (first 15% of the first 15% of the first 15%). We can clearly define what you missed in your CX process, what the No.1 area of service variation is, and the impact this has on your market. When we talk about understanding your CX and its impact on your market, this is what we mean.

Online, SMS and paper-based surveys will never give you the precise data you need to define your CX process to the No.1 position. It will tell you a whole lot of **what** but it will never tell you **why**.

This is the secret weapon No.1 companies have over their market — they are using the right metrics to know the WHY.

Chapter 5
Commandment IV
ANALYSE YOUR CX BUCKET

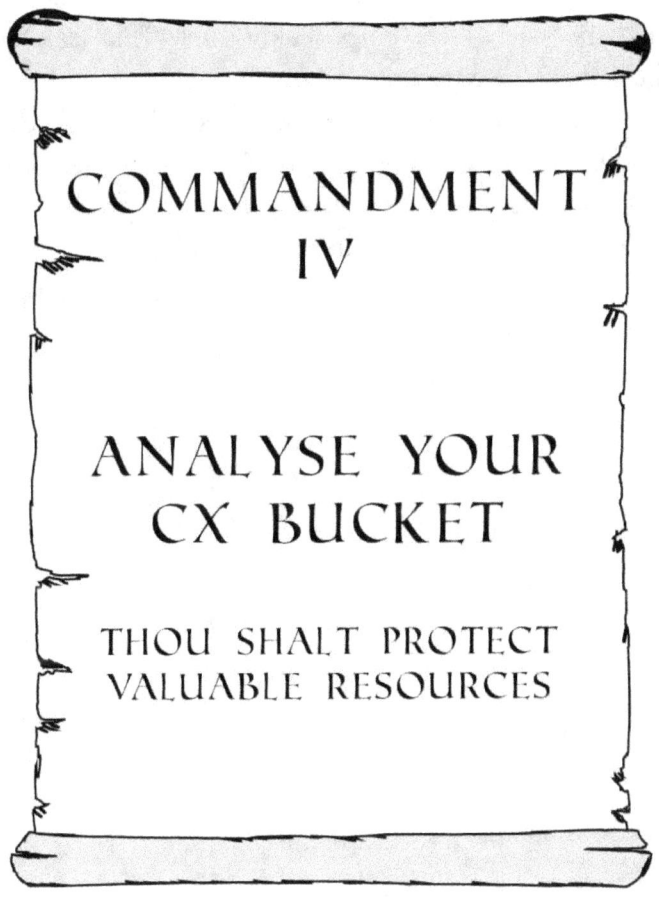

COMMANDMENT
IV

ANALYSE YOUR
CX BUCKET

THOU SHALT PROTECT
VALUABLE RESOURCES

How much water would it take to fill up a bucket with many holes?

An unlimited supply.

The water level will be determined by the flow rate in and the size of the holes leaking out. This leaking bucket can be compared to how a client base works, a CX bucket. Your marketing investment is the inflow of new prospects and repeat clients into your CX bucket. The effectiveness of your CX process (a combination of the quality of your touchpoints and your first 15% processes) will determine how many, what size and what type of leakage you have.

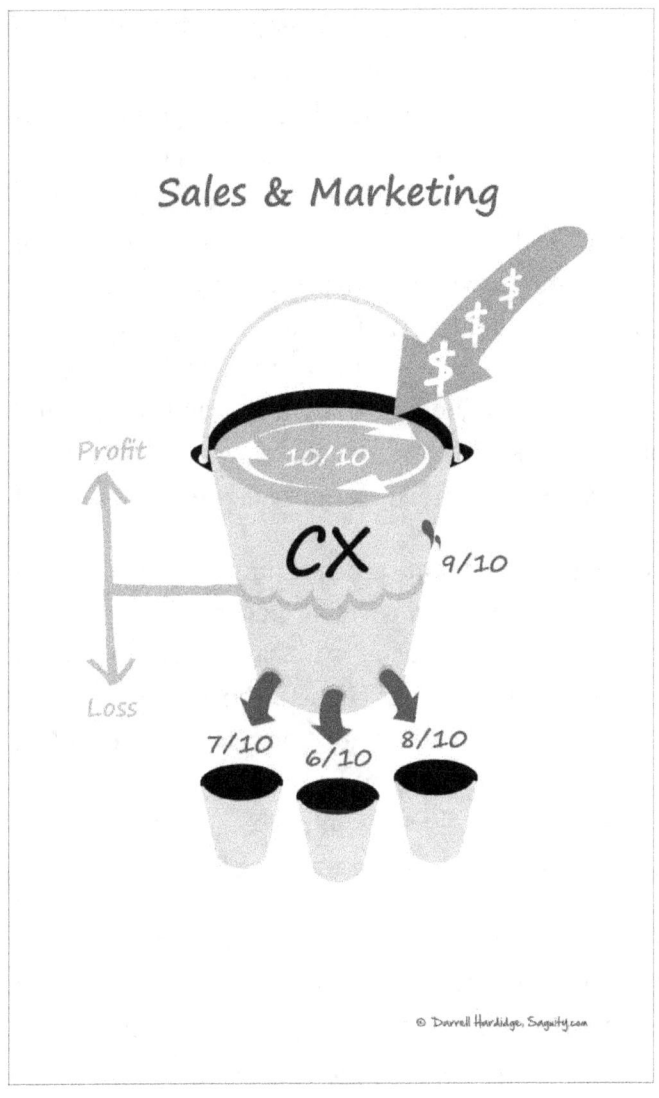

If you have an excellent CX process, the integrity of your CX bucket will be strong. The level of marketing flow-in can be adjusted to suit the demand you choose to have (ideal scenario). This is usually identified by a company that does not advertise special deals or sales in order to generate demand. No. 1 companies keep their edge by educating and innovating their CX, and rarely worry about the competition. The opportunity with this CX edge is you can either increase flow to expand the business or determine the type of market you want to serve. This results in optimal margins and profits.

Alternatively, if you are like most companies, you will have a percentage of leakage and you have to keep chasing new business to stay ahead of the churn rate (to replenish lost clients who no longer chose you). There is a natural attrition rate to be considered — for example, it's a bit hard to sell another pram to a parent with a five-year-old (as they mature out of your market), but I'm not referring to this.

A big mistake many companies make is confusing the attrition rate with the actual churn rate. This causes them to miss a massive opportunity to reduce the waste of cashflow, profits, resources, marketing efforts, and core business focus.

Chapter 5: Commandment IV – ANALYSE YOUR CX BUCKET

Recently, we researched the CX of a company and discovered they had major holes in their CX bucket. They incentivised the sales and marketing teams with bonuses on new client acquisition and had no focus at all on client retention (a major breakdown in CX touchpoint management). To our amazement, no one was responsible for ensuring client loyalty.

How can such a massive mistake be made? It's crazy to invest heavily in turning on the tap faster, yet do nothing about plugging the leaks that are pouring out huge amounts of cash.

As the diagram shows, each hole gets bigger as you go down. The one at the top is small, the next one down is slightly bigger, and each one gets even bigger as it gets lower. Starting from the top, each of those holes represents your CX scores out of 10. The smallest one is your 9/10 clients. Next is 8/10 and so on. Even with a 9/10 client appreciation score, you're still losing clients to competition as you haven't optimised (improved) your relationship with them. You might think these losses are tolerable, that your bucket isn't leaking so badly and you have high loyalty. The real test to sort out this theory: stop marketing entirely and see if your bucket stays full. In all likelihood, these leaks are significant — your marketing is all that's stemming the flow and it's very expensive.

The first and most obvious solution companies jump on is their marketing budget. If you increase the marketing budget, you bring in more clients. It's a simple, short-term solution but it lacks effectiveness. When you simply spend money on marketing to bring in new bodies, all you do is align the new clients up with the appropriate hole to leak back out of the bucket again. This isn't optimisation; it's a blunt force solution of trying to cram the bucket full rather than finding out why there are holes. Not only are you still losing clients, you're spending a fortune on marketing to ineffectively refill your bucket, losing even more money in the process.

It's at least six times more expensive to buy a new client than have an existing one return.

Most companies have a client acquisition budget. Very few have a client retention budget, and this is often where the greatest ROI exists. It's not very exciting for the marketing and sales team, but is very exciting for shareholders. When retention is increased, it leads to greater revenue and profits.

Chapter 5: Commandment IV – ANALYSE YOUR CX
BUCKET

The better solution is to optimise your client experience process and enjoy repeat spending and referrals by diminishing the holes in your CX bucket. Your 10/10 appreciative clients are those who always stay in the bucket. These are your truly loyal clients. Not only do they stay in the bucket, they continue to fill it with their repeat transactions. These 10/10 clients are a constant source of income. Their loyalty keeps them coming back and they refer new clients. These new clients will come in with the best impression of you. It's easier to try to plug the gaps with marketing campaigns (a Band-Aid), but **it's much harder optimising your company's practices so the holes don't occur at all.** The rewards for doing this so far outweigh the easy marketing solution.

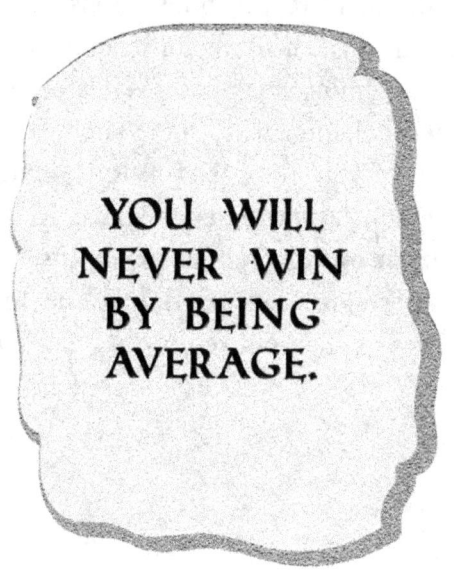

YOU WILL
NEVER WIN
BY BEING
AVERAGE.

Chapter 5: Commandment IV – ANALYSE YOUR CX BUCKET

At Saguity we've proven with our clients, the higher your level of CX optimisation, the fewer holes you have in your bucket and the more profit you make. We conduct independent research on what caused the holes, and what causes the appreciation and loyalty from your 10/10 clients. We find ways to bring the low scoring clients up to join the higher scores. If your business maintains a stronger level of 9/10 and 10/10 appreciation scores from clients, you'll be saving a fortune on your marketing budget. Your client referral rate and return business keeps filling the bucket. This is why it's imperative to **never stop optimising** your CX process to get every client possible to a 10/10 client appreciation level.

The only way to determine the integrity of your CX bucket is to have the correct KPIs and the correct process to investigate. Rarely do we see a new client who has this in play.

How many buckets do you have? If you have multiple locations, dealerships, franchises, sales people, then you have multiple buckets, and we know that you will have a large degree of variation between them. This in itself is a game-changer for many and the immediate opportunity to improve revenue and profits. Many of our clients with multiple locations use our Client Appreciation Index as a KPI in their business reporting. Those who do are thriving.

Chapter 6
Commandment V
MASTER THE GOLDEN RULE OF RESPONSIBILITY

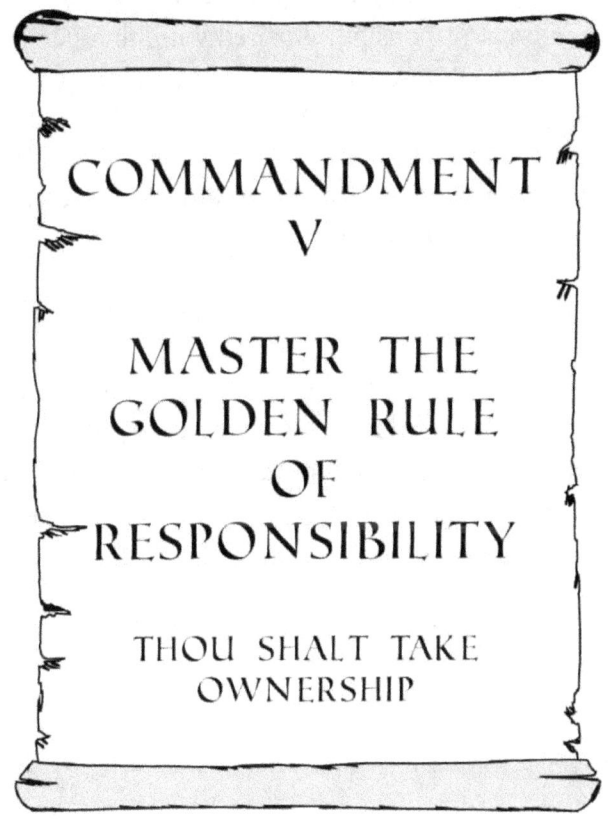

Internal Responsibility is your secret weapon to optimising team performance. Business leaders know their teams play a critical role in the success of the business and delivery of client experience. Many struggle with knowing how to implement and sustain a great team culture that has a clear focus on optimising CX. Ideally, everyone in a business would have internal responsibility paired with high personal motivation and desire to serve. But this isn't always the case.

Getting your team to have 'internal responsibility' as a baseline commitment is possible.

But what does this mean when it comes to CX?

Internal responsibility is driven by inspiration to take initiative and do whatever it takes to be of service. External responsibility requires constant motivation to get people to go beyond the basics. Every…Single…Time.

LEAVE IT
WITH ME,
I'LL TAKE
CARE
OF IT.

Chapter 6: Commandment V– MASTER THE GOLDEN RULE OF RESPONSIBILITY

With internal responsibility, team members approach any client request or issue with the mindset of 'Leave it with me, I'll take care of it.' As consumers, when we believe a company we deal with has this commitment and delivers upon it, it creates a subconscious automatic bias towards this business. It gives us confidence and trust in the ability of that company to provide exceptional quality.

The desire of an individual's commitment to serve on behalf of their company is more powerful than any staff behavioural or moral code. It's innate and doesn't require external pressure or motivation. It's a self-generating behaviour. When internal responsibility is the foundation of the team culture, it builds a powerhouse that has enormous strength and resilience to overcome the greatest of challenges.

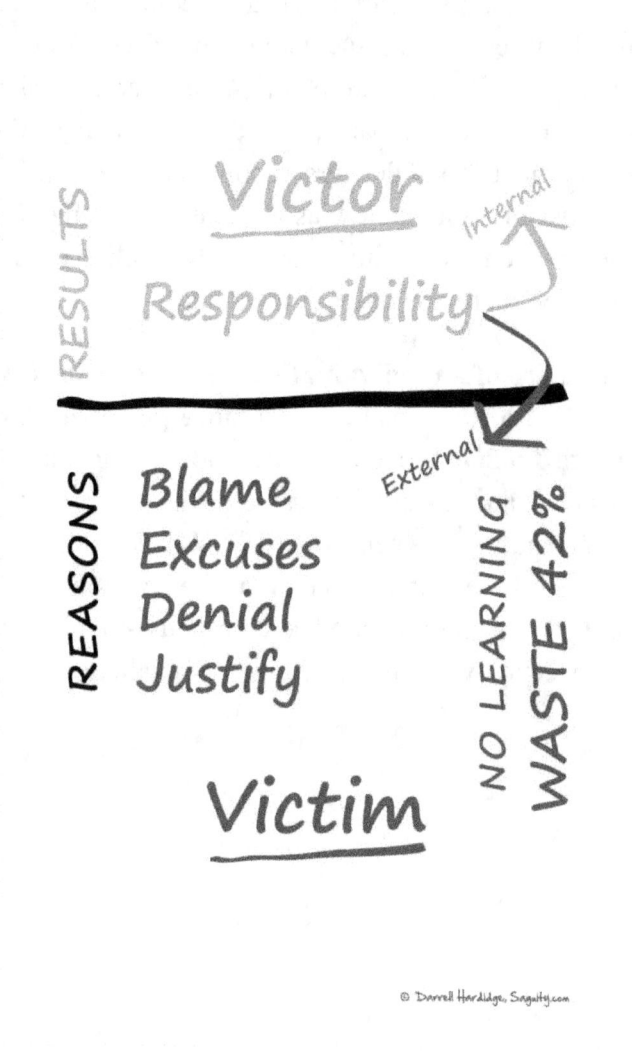

Chapter 6: Commandment V– MASTER THE GOLDEN RULE OF RESPONSIBILITY

Some of your team members may not be using their full potential. They need encouragement to draw out their own sense of internal responsibility. You purchase 38 hours of their time every week, so why not invest in ensuring as much of it as possible is committed to being above the line?

Dr Deming determined that up to 42% of waste is attributed to below the line behaviour. Every step you take towards moving your culture above the line will pay huge dividends.

Many companies and employees go below-the-line into blame, excuses, denial and justification. They say to clients, 'That's not my department', 'It's company policy', 'We don't do that' or 'Call back tomorrow' — the list is endless and the damage to trust held by the clients can go deep and permanent.

These are common excuses team members make. The real concern is their leadership accepts it. They say the same things and therefore set the standard that below-the-line behaviour is accepted. Look closer and you will see where the cracks start.

No.1 companies have a 'Leave it with me; I'll take care of it' attitude from top to bottom. This simple statement defines the core behaviour of every individual and defines the DNA of the company. The essence of this statement declares, 'I'll do whatever I can, to the best of my ability, and if I can't fulfil the request, I'll find someone who will'. The alternative is team members taking the easy road and passing the buck, leaving an unfulfilled client who now has to source other suppliers to solve their problem. This attitude costs you in wallet-share and is very likely creating detractors of your company.

INTERNAL
RESPONSIBILITY
IS THE
ESSENCE
OF
INTEGRITY.

Chapter 6: Commandment V– MASTER THE GOLDEN RULE OF RESPONSIBILITY

Without internal responsibility as the core of your cultural commitment, you cannot achieve extreme client loyalty and a high degree of market relevance. At best, you will deliver a standard of satisfaction — and satisfaction does not create loyalty. It will lead your company into the fog of irrelevance.

The Two-Buck Rule

A client had an open discussion with his team about operating 'above the line' and 'internal responsibility'. The CEO decided to implement the two-buck rule. He put a jar in the office, and if a team member had wasted time by 'laying blame, justifying or making excuses', the member would have to put $2 in the jar. At the end of the first week, the jar held $280 from a team of 35 people (the money was given to charity). Those who repetitively played 'below the line' became more apparent, and more disgruntled and annoyed. Those who played 'above the line' lifted team spirits and were happier, with more fulfilment in their role. A few of the team commented they'd taken the principle home to their kids and were having great success with it.

Below-the-line players were really struggling with the change in environment and the new vibe of the team. They couldn't default back to their old ways, and some people couldn't adapt to the constant improvements, so a couple of them quit their roles! The CEO noted how much of a drain the below-the-line mindset was on the business. They had become accustomed to accepting average as a standard for their business culture.

Just as 'like attracts like', the replacement people were 'above-the-line' players who were attracted to the ideals the CEO projected into their company. This principle creates a space for better individuals to join the team and better serve their market.

Try the Two-Buck Rule yourself and have some fun with it. It will shift the vibe of your team like you will not believe. You will be amazed at how quickly change will occur in areas you have struggled with for a long time.

This commandment will elevate your team culture and improve your business with increased client loyalty and accountability. Your team will continue to evolve to greater standards of client experience. The golden rule of responsibility is absolutely critical if you want to optimise your touchpoints, master your first 15%, plug the holes in your CX bucket, and have real purpose behind your WHY.

Chapter 7
Commandment VI
GO BEYOND EXPECTATIONS

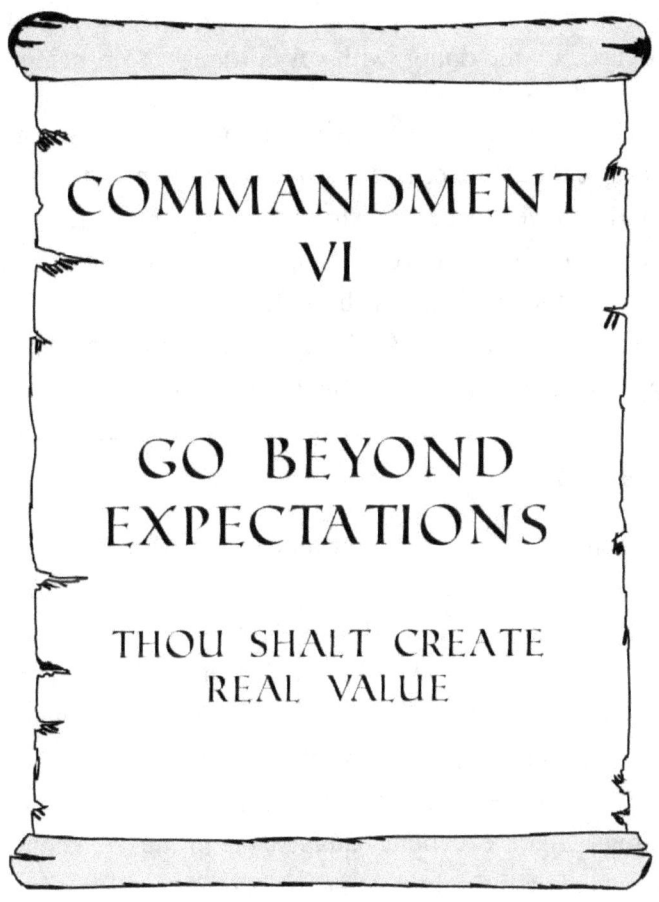

Have you ever had the experience of being served with a predictable process that ticks all the boxes? You got what you needed but nothing more, and it was all a bit mechanical. They didn't do anything wrong but you felt like you were just transacted and not served. Sometimes the CX training is too highly focused on the **do**ing, with very little focus on **be**ing.

It's vital to have processes and systems working, and your team capable. But this is not enough in today's marketplace to create extreme loyalty. You have to know how to go beyond people's expectations. This is often the challenge with the first 15% process: how do you humanise it? At the end of the day, we are all people. Courtesy, a smile with a genuine 'thank you', and a commitment to being of service goes a very long way.

Imagine I'm at a function and I meet three of your best clients. I just so happen to be looking for a new supplier in your field. In conversation, they tell me about you and I ask, 'Aren't they all the same, the last one said they were the best?' As an extremely loyal client does, they go into bat for you. They tell me all the reasons why they are happy. They say things like excellent quality, helpfulness, being knowledgeable, always having stock, good pricing, experience, understanding them, reliability, and being on time, friendly, efficient, supportive, etc.

Quality   Good price
Friendly   Helpful
Knowledge   Stock
Diverse produce range
Understanding needs
Team   Empathy
Nice   On time
&   Delivery
Easy   Know me
Communication
Solutions   Integrity
Great Value   Support
Responsible   Quick
Convenience   Location
Parking   Loyalty
Skill   Innovation

TRUST

EXPECTED

satisfied

© Darrell Hardidge, Saguity.com

Chapter 7: Commandment VI – GO BEYOND EXPECTATIONS

This all sounds great and it's impressive, but I have a simple question: *As opposed to what?* Poor quality, unhelpful, no knowledge, no stock, a rip-off, no experience, misunderstood, late, rude, disorganised, no care?

All the positive things your clients said to me are totally EXPECTED, and why? Because the alternative is unacceptable.

JUST GIVING
CLIENTS WHAT
THEY WANT IS
NOT ENOUGH
IF YOU WANT
THE EXCLUSIVE
SUPPLY OF
THEIR WALLET.

Chapter 7: Commandment VI – GO BEYOND
EXPECTATIONS

This is an issue for many companies. They firmly believe if you give people what they expect, you will earn their loyalty. The reality is that expectation is just the start of the journey. If that's all you do, then you better have a prime location, exclusive supply, or something that protects you.

Consider the recent innovations of Alibaba, Airbnb, and Uber as examples of the changes that are coming. How is the disruption going to impact your company? It's not if, but when.

The one thing that stands the test of time and is your last bastion of protection *is excellent service*. The crazy thing is it's the cheapest strategy to implement. The massive returns it gives keep on giving. Your market is more impatient than ever. If there is a lack of human connection from your team to your market, you will become no more than a commodity. This will always keep you in the Price Trap.

A big challenge with shifting the team culture of CX into a mindset of excellence is the leadership and their beliefs. Too often they are driven by KPIs and budgets. The main connection they have with their market is a financial one. This is vital, but what's missing is the emotional connection (heart drivers), which is also known as the 'soft connection'. The usual KPIs are the hard connection. In these situations, the leadership doesn't have any KPIs to accurately measure their client experience and engagement.

Many times, I have experienced the leadership having no idea what the key heart drivers are for their clients' loyalty. Nor can they define the behaviours that lead the market to select them over the competition. Very few companies know how to design a heart connection CX process, so they use consultants and other market templates that are vague and inaccurate.

SATISFACTION
IS FINISHED.
IT WILL TRAP
YOU INTO A
FALSE SENSE
OF SECURITY.

Chapter 7: Commandment VI – GO BEYOND EXPECTATIONS

Do you want to be common and same-same? Or do you want to be unique? You can never design a unique CX process if the foundation is based on the standards of others. You are unique and you do have a point of difference. The secret is in knowing how to find it. The answer is always within your clients' expression based upon their values and beliefs. This is what we at Saguity find out in our CX research. It's a bullet-proof strategy and designed by those who support you with their loyalty.

Your commitment to 'going beyond the expected' is your point of empowerment. It's when the opinions and biases of your team have been removed and their minds are open to exploring new ways of thinking. This provides the opportunity to start with a blank canvas and create a unique CX process. The key is removing the 'I KNOW' attitude. It's about being a 'Learner, not a Knower'. Most importantly, it's about not being scared that you don't know the answer. Don't see errors as mistakes, rather see them as a 'mis-take'. Think of the movies, take 1, take 2…take 15; it's all about getting it right and rarely is it on take 1. So why do businesses think they have to get the movie perfect on take 1?

Chapter 8
Commandment VII
STAY OUT OF THE FOG

COMMANDMENT VII

STAY OUT OF THE FOG

THOU SHALT DISCOVER HOW TO BE RELEVANT

A word you can associate with fog is 'uncertainty'. Think of driving in fog. One moment you can see and are in control. The next you're in the thick of it, on the edge of danger and uncertainty. Business can be the same: one quarter it's all going to plan, then unexpectedly, a few key clients slow down or stop spending. Perhaps the marketing campaign isn't working to plan and the budgets have gone south. Often the reasons why are incorrectly understood.

When we have interviewed clients who have defected, we find the real reasons why they left. Their responses are completely different to what the business believed. More surprising is how often the businesses have never inquired to find out *why* the clients stopped buying. Instead, they just focus on finding new clients. The worst thing about this situation is that commissions and bonuses are paid for client acquisition to replace the leakage due to bad service.

Instead of plugging the holes in their CX bucket, these businesses turn the marketing tap on harder, hoping it will fix the problem. It never does. It's a Band-Aid and only hurts the bottom line. Often what's overlooked is the cost of human resources to manage the on-boarding of a new client. Revenue is up but profits are down.

When it comes to client experience, there is one very clear and simple fact, 'If you're not remarkable, you're invisible: if you don't stand out, you're irrelevant'.

The fog is like a bad headache for business. It saps the energy, time and attention of your team. The focus on how to navigate business in the fog is like driving your car in the fog with no map or directions. You lose the ability to control your resources and your strategy to optimise sales and margins. Most of the time, no matter what you do, you end up back at the same point you started or, worse still, lost.

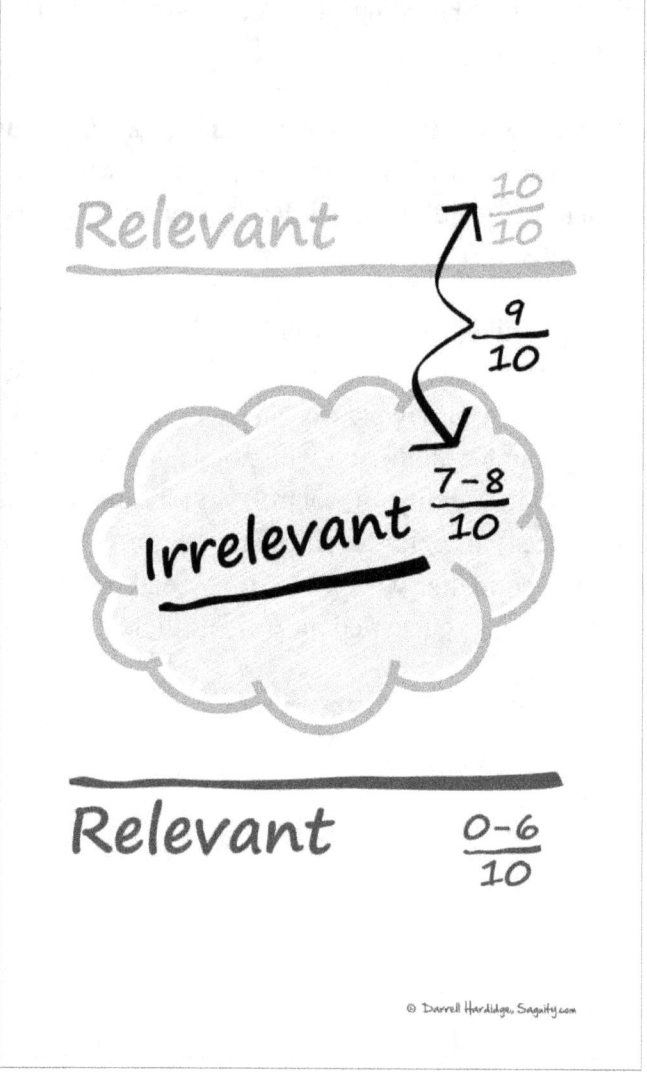

Relevant $\frac{10}{10}$

$\frac{9}{10}$

Irrelevant $\frac{7-8}{10}$

Relevant $\frac{0-6}{10}$

© Darrell Hardidge, Saguity.com

Chapter 8: Commandment VII – STAY OUT OF THE FOG

So many sales and marketing managers are lost in the fog of irrelevance. They obsess over their competitors and try to outdo them. They have small wins, but are constantly operating in a state of uncertainty. Leading companies do the opposite; they obsess over their clients. They constantly innovate and focus on how to improve their service standards. They accurately measure their CX with the correct information to ensure they keep highly relevant to their market.

YOU MUST
OBSESS OVER
YOUR CLIENTS
AND NOT
OVER YOUR
COMPETITORS.

Chapter 8: Commandment VII – STAY OUT OF THE FOG

Think of all the businesses you have personally dealt with over the last six months. Now think about how many transactions truly stood out and were remarkable in their service experience. This is where you felt truly appreciated and respected for your business. For those that stood out, isn't it likely you would definitely use their services again before considering anyone else. It's also more likely you'd put your personal reputation on the line and recommend them to a friend or colleague.

The interesting question here is the percentage. What is the percentage of businesses that exist in your circle of choice? These are the ones that are relevant to you. I have posed this question to thousands of people in my keynotes and workshops, and the average number of businesses that have high relevance (really stand out) is on average 15%. This means the other 85% are irrelevant and must consistently find new ways to re-engage with you. If they don't, you never give them a second thought and may never use them again.

If you want to find one specific point of difference between a leading company and a competitive one, it's in a simple but complex KPI. Very few companies have worked out how to implement an accurate KPI for measuring their CX and their market relevance. Most are relying on financial data that's historic. P&L and cashflow are based on what happened, not what will happen. Even cashflow forecasting relies on a combination of opinion, client contracts, and orders. Beyond that, what do they have?

Saguity's Client Appreciation Index (CAI™) measures the critical factors of client experience and the vital driver of your emotional relationship to your market. If you don't have accurate KPIs on CX, you are operating your business in the fog of irrelevance. Measuring client experience and having an ongoing benchmarking process is vital for ensuring you stay relevant to your clients. No one can afford to guess, but that's what most companies are doing. **There is a reason there are only a few at the front of every market. They lead the way simply because they know what their clients want more than their competitors do.**

THERE ARE NO
TRUE LEADERS
IN A
COMPETITIVE
MARKET WHO
HAVE AVERAGE
SERVICE. THE
IMMUTABLE LAWS
OF BUSINESS
WILL NOT
ALLOW IT.

Chapter 8: Commandment VII – STAY OUT OF THE FOG

Your mission is to understand your client's emotional connection with you.

When you know WHY they think the way they do and WHY you are relevant to them, you will have very precise data to create and support your CX strategy. Most companies are using inaccurate and re-active online data that only tell them the basics of WHAT they think with no insights into WHY. The scary reality is most companies are driving using their rear-view mirror. They are making decisions on where they are going with very poor client information.

Chapter 9
Commandment VIII
UNDERSTAND THE POWER
OF APPRECIATION

COMMANDMENT
VIII

UNDERSTAND
THE POWER OF
APPRECIATION

THOU SHALT ALWAYS
BE APPRECIATED

Think back to when you were at school. If you got an 8/10 (usually given as a B or B+), how well would you have done at graduation? You would have easily passed and in general been a great student. For the bulk of society, our education experience has trained us to think that 5/10 is a pass and 8/10 is a great result. This belief has been transferred into day-to-day life. Businesses also think an 8/10 is a measurement of success. You can get into a university with an 8/10. But to get into the No.1 university you need at least a 9/10, and then it's still just a chance. To be certain, you need a 10/10. **The best of the best demands a 10/10.**

Not aiming for a 10/10 CX score is a fundamental error that most businesses make, and it costs them a fortune. Not because they don't care or aren't committed, but simply, a lack of understanding. In business, if you have an average CX score of 8/10, it's considered a 'job well done' and you have achieved a great standard of satisfaction and loyalty. This is a false reality. Every day we are conditioned to believe it. However, the leading companies have a secret you don't know about. They have a game plan that keeps them highly relevant to their market. Knowledge is power, and leading companies understand their clients, so they have information that's significantly more insightful than their competitors have.

Have you noticed how service excellence awards are given and what company success statements are based upon?

Consider the amount of times you hear or read about 100% satisfaction. Marketing blasts it at us everywhere: the '100% satisfaction guarantee', 'you will be 100% satisfied', 'our satisfaction ratings are the highest', I could go on and on. All this says is: you will be fine, OK, mostly happy, and generally get what you want. Nothing can be further from the truth when it comes to mastering CX and earning the right to extreme loyalty.

MEASURING SATISFACTION AS A KPI WILL KEEP YOU IRRELEVANT AND CONSISTENTLY REQUIRE YOU TO RE-ENGAGE WITH YOUR MARKET.

Chapter 9: Commandment VIII – UNDERSTAND THE POWER OF APPRECIATION

This misleading measurement of satisfaction costs a fortune in lost opportunity. You are constantly having to refill your CX bucket because clients have chosen to share their wallet with your competitors. It's vital you understand the CAI™. This is the new way of thinking for strategy and measurement of CX. Our clients have a secret weapon. They have clarity and precision in knowing what to focus on and this sets them apart. They use the CAI™ and have more understanding and knowledge of their clients and their values than ever before.

Remember how you feel when you are truly appreciative of someone?

You trust them, you care for them, you respect them, and you support them. You will do far more for someone you appreciate than someone you are generally satisfied with. This is the identity that leading companies go to painstaking lengths to discover and to protect. If you aren't appreciated, you're irrelevant.

WHEN IT
COMES TO
BEING Nº 1
THERE IS
NO FINISH
LINE.

Chapter 9: Commandment VIII – UNDERSTAND THE POWER OF APPRECIATION

Leading companies have a very simple philosophy around their CX process. They believe, **'When it comes to being No.1, there is no finish line'**. At Saguity, we operate at a level of, **'Last week's standard is no longer acceptable'**. Innovation is not an intention; it must be the driving force behind everything you do. When it comes to innovation in CX, our research defines this as, 'change that adds optimal client value'. Everything you do with innovation must include how it impacts your CX process. Client centricity has your clients at the core of everything you do. As I explained in Commandment 2, 'Mastering the CX Journey', everything speaks and everything leads to the tip of the arrow, impacting on client experience.

One of Dr Deming's principles defines the foundations of quality. We have adapted this into the Saguity analytic process and strategic reporting. While it's a simple principle to observe, it's the most challenging to achieve. Leading companies never lose focus of this principle. It defines who they are and their cultural values. Saguity's research has proven its accuracy and relationship with market dominance and profitability to such a degree that we call it an 'immutable law of business'.

This is the foundation of our unique measurement that defines service excellence in CX, known as Appreciation Certified™. The confirmation that a company has achieved an extreme standard of service excellence that is independently backed by an assessment of their markets feedback. (Go to saguity.com to understand more about the new standard that defines service excellence and what it means to achieve it).

The Golden
Rule of
Client Experience

MAX Client
Appreciation

―――――――――――

MIN Variation

© Darrell Hardidge, Saguity.com

The No.1 rule of CX comes down to a very clear and precise formula. Just like $E=mc^2$, it doesn't give any indication of how hard it is to define.

Understand this principle and take action to get it in your company. It will define how you operate and it will humanise quality as a cultural behaviour. It's essential this principle becomes a vital foundation in all your company dialogue. Your team needs to use this principle whenever there is innovation, implementation, or just discussion of operational issues.

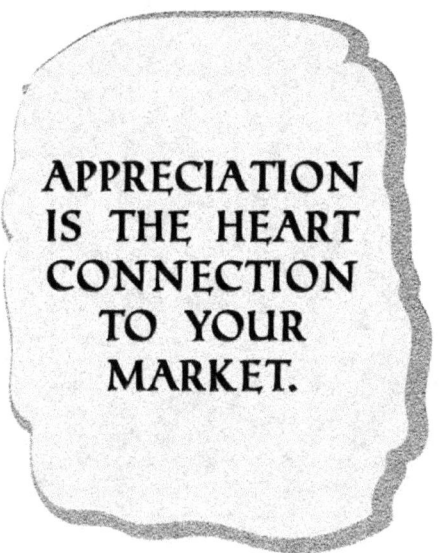

APPRECIATION
IS THE HEART
CONNECTION
TO YOUR
MARKET.

Chapter 9: Commandment VIII – UNDERSTAND THE POWER OF APPRECIATION

Our clients make this an essential part of their focus. They constantly search for ways to reduce variation in their CX process. It doesn't matter which area of your company you apply it to, reducing variation will always pay big dividends.

Look at all the touchpoints in your CX journey, then apply this principle. Consider the on-boarding of a new client. How do you ensure there is no variation in their experience across your touchpoints? There is no prize for getting most of the process right if your delivery is late or wrong. Anywhere there is variation in your CX process will impact on your CX score and your client loyalty.

Every time you innovate and reduce service variation, you immediately increase client appreciation. These two factors are directly proportional to client experience and revenue. You will never see a No.1 company with maximum margins operating in a state of variation. Every process you have in your business needs to follow this Deming principle. Look at your touchpoints, dig into the first 15%, and optimise your processes to reduce variation.

Reducing variation has a huge impact on the efficiency and retention of human resources. The amount of time wasted on resolving errors from variation costs a lot more than money. It has a big impact on your CX process and, therefore, your degree of relevance to your market.

EVERYONE IS
RESPONSIBLE
FOR CLIENT
EXPERIENCE
AND FOR
CREATING A
10/10 SERVICE
CULTURE.

Chapter 9: Commandment VIII – UNDERSTAND THE POWER OF APPRECIATION

Profit margins are directly proportional to the degree of variation you have in your CX process. We are often surprised at how many companies and their senior executives have absolutely no awareness of this principle. Without this principle in play, there is certainty your profits are reduced. What's more surprising is the short-sightedness of so many companies that focus on the quick fix (which never is) and cannot see the benefit of investing in quality CX research that provides an ultra-clear road map to reducing variation and maximising profits.

Leading companies walk the walk and see their CX process as a vital KPI in their strategy and reporting. Having your sales, marketing, account management, operations, delivery etc. included in these KPIs will ensure a focus across all your touchpoints. Everyone in your company is responsible for client experience. Having every department focus on reducing their variation and waste will dramatically affect your degree of market relevance. Your clients want to see it and experience it; they don't want to hear about it.

Chapter 10
Commandment IX
AVOID THE PRICE TRAP

COMMANDMENT
IX

AVOID THE
PRICE TRAP

THOU SHALT
BECOME UNIQUE

There are certain businesses that operate at the top of the price point and continue to grow while their competitors cut prices to get market share yet rarely put a dent in the top operator. This occurs at the very high end of the market and at the high-transaction end. In any market, there are always leaders and followers. On the surface, it can be hard to pinpoint where the differentiator is; however, the demand from the marketplace states they are doing something different. A statement I use for this commandment is:

Different isn't always better, but better is always different.

So many companies try to be 'different' in order to have significance. It's often short lived as the competition just throws another curve ball and it starts all over again. So much money is wasted on gimmicks and deals trying to be different thinking this will build loyalty. While it can have an impact, it's often a short spike and it usually costs margin. The question to consider is whether you want market share or wallet share the most? Market share can really stress resources and requires significant effort; whereas, wallet share enables a lot more choice and the ability to optimise strategy. Your particular business model does a have a lot to do with which one is preferable, but there are some that dominate both market share and wallet share.

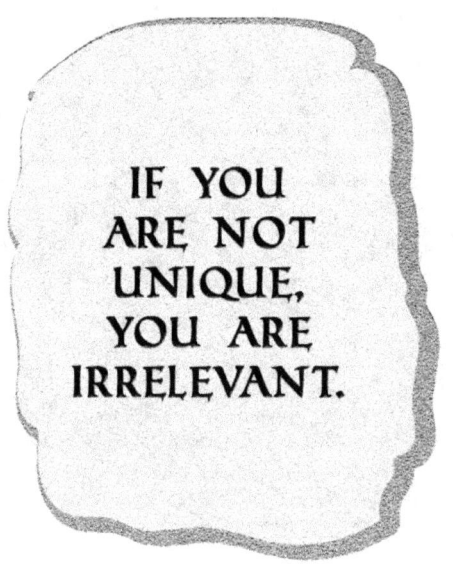

IF YOU
ARE NOT
UNIQUE,
YOU ARE
IRRELEVANT.

Chapter 10: Commandment IX – AVOID THE PRICE TRAP

Being 'better' is a totally different game plan. There is no luck in right time, right place, and right market for achieving excellence. At Saguity, we have the privilege of working with some of Australia's great companies who are totally masterful in delivering service excellence.

These No.1 companies have this process so defined they can accurately predict how their CX will be in all their touchpoints. This ensures they have the highest degree of market relevance. The first 15% is the DNA of their business systems: it's automatic, it's immediate thinking, and nothing is left to chance. Their history has taught them how to arm themselves with backup processes to handle the 'just in case scenario'.

We have over 300,000 client interviews on file in our data warehouse. All of them are managed to a specific process that enables segmentation and analysis across multiple fields and industries. The proof is in the numbers. **The market never lies; it always behaves exactly in proportion to how well you respect it and how well you serve it**.

There is a misconception that market forces always drive prices. While price must be carefully monitored, as it's definitely affected by efficiency and supply, there is another force behind price that has been there from the very beginning of competition. Very few companies have a clear and unbiased strategy to enable them to see opportunity. For many it's right there in front of them and they have not been able to see it. If you have the wrong theory, it doesn't matter how hard you try and how specific you are, you'll never achieve the optimal outcome.

IF YOUR
CLIENTS
ARE MERELY
SATISFIED
THEN IT'S
ALL ABOUT
PRICE.

Chapter 10: Commandment IX – AVOID THE PRICE TRAP

Look at the companies you deal with and think about their delivery on product or service. Is most of it predictable? As I mentioned in Commandment 6, 'Beyond Expected', there isn't much of a difference between competitors. This is the challenge for those who don't innovate their CX process. Innovation has a very specific distinction when it applies to CX, yet very few understand it. Some do it by instinct, but the No.1 companies have a very clear and precise planning process.

We have tens of thousands of perfect CX scores of 10/10 in our data warehouse. This proves beyond doubt that smart operators know how to leverage innovation. Innovation by our distinction means 'change that adds optimal client value'. Sounds simple, but unless you know how to accurately measure client value (that is, what 'they say' is of great value), then you will probably have the wrong strategy, because it's based on the wrong theory to start with. Most companies make the error of determining internally what client value is, and this has bias written all over it.

The Price Trap is where you are stuck competing on price. It's like a very slippery icy road. If you don't take care, it could cause you some serious damage which can be fatal. There are plenty of companies that were extremely busy and looked great on the surface, but went bust in a ball of flames and became another statistic. In many cases, the cause was lack of margin due to being caught in the Price Trap and not knowing how to escape. Many could have recovered had they been able to redefine their value and optimise their CX process.

The diagram below is a simple example of what happens with the Price Trap. Every company offers either a product or service, some have both. If you are price focused, it's fast paced and very disruptive. You must constantly monitor the competition and adjust. In these situations, margins are squeezed and cashflow is the objective. The focus here is how to reduce costs to increase margins. Labour costs are usually the prime target as they have an immediate impact on the bottom line. You can keep stock to sell for another day but you can't sell last week's labour.

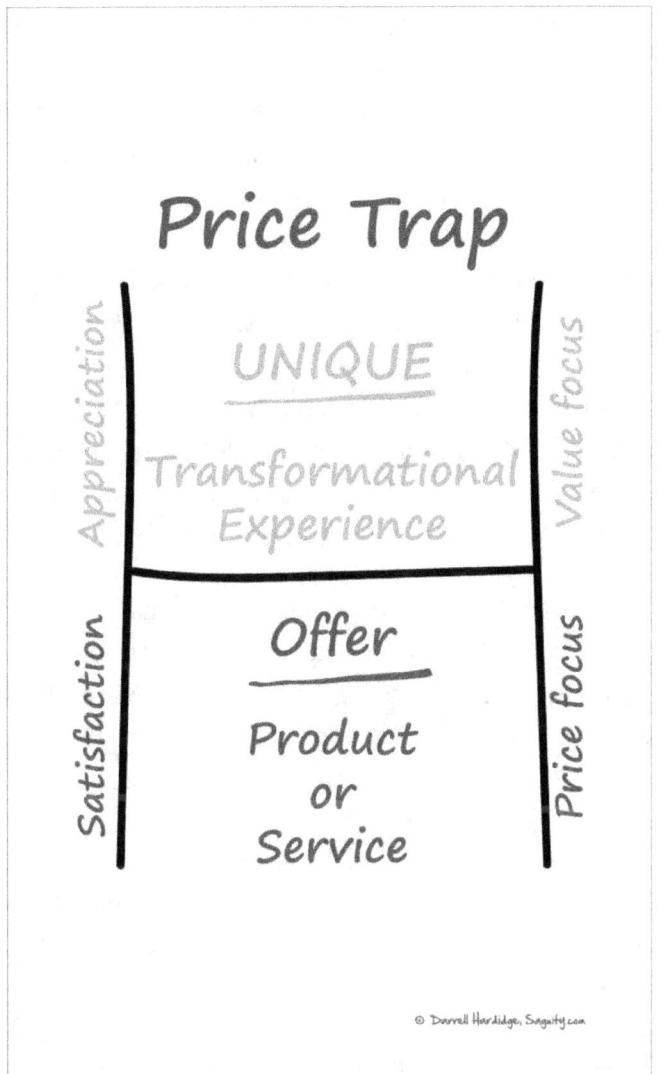

How many times have you been into a store and been made to wait? Others are waiting and some walk out. Some choose to only buy the minimum, and rarely is there time for the sales team to offer any quality service. As a result, the store sells a lot less than it could have and clients are frustrated. At best, you have a client base that's barely satisfied and not loyal. However, internally, the company will view the market as being 'tough' and believe they cannot optimise margins. It's amazing how the answer is so apparent, yet the decisions are made from head office by people who never get behind the counter or go onsite to understand what the real problem is.

There is another area often overlooked that is a huge profit maker. The answers are immediate if you know what the questions are. **Rarely does a company look to its clients for the answers to their challenges**. The reasons range from ignorance and ego to not knowing how to get the correct and appropriate information. Knowledge is power and it's a very valuable currency to a company. It is vital to its success, yet so many fly blind when designing their optimal CX process.

The source of critical knowledge and information is within your client base. Not just any client base: it's

the ones who score you a perfect 10/10 for CX. These
clients are your most valuable asset and your golden
toolbox for innovation. With the correct process for
researching your market, you can discover what
makes you unique, what makes you different, and
what makes you better. However, the critical factor in
understanding your uniqueness lies in a greater
distinction. Very few companies are able to discover
the true essence of what sets them apart and,
therefore, miss the bullseye.

The answer to your uniqueness, your point of
difference, and what makes you better, exists in the
heart drivers to your greatest client discovery. It's
about WHY you are unique. Delivering
transformational experiences creates a completely
new distinction of value that's beyond the ability of
your competitors.

ONLY YOUR
CLIENTS CAN
TELL YOU
WHAT MAKES
YOU
UNIQUE.

Chapter 10: Commandment IX – AVOID THE PRICE TRAP

If you don't discover what makes you unique directly from your clients, the only available options are guessing, internal opinion, generic market data and your competition. All of these are flawed, can guide you the wrong way, and inevitably waste a lot of money, time, and, most importantly, wallet share. When you define your uniqueness with your own 10/10 clients, you have **extreme client loyalty**, which is the most powerful rocket fuel available.

Getting out of the Price Trap can only be achieved by defining your uniqueness in a very specific and certain way. You won't find this information from your web-based, email, SMS, or paper-based research programs. It can only be achieved by having a real-time conversation that's precise and structured to a specific outcome. Companies struggle to define their uniqueness because they are using the wrong theory and the wrong process, which means they end up with wrong, often useless information.

The Saguity methodology uses real time phone conversations to determine your uniqueness and your WHY. We have proven many times that the online-based CX programs are flawed. Often these flaws are from the way they are implemented and the inexperience of who is managing them.

You do what you do to the best of your ability and we do the same. We ONLY focus on CX research and process and what drives your edge. We don't do finance, IT, construction, retail, or automotive, etc. That's what our clients do and we help them master their CX process. If you want to know how to get out of the Price Trap, then use an expert who can define WHY you're in it in the first place. If your current team or CX strategist can't explain WHY, then you're using the wrong methodology around measuring CX and definitely losing revenue and margin.

Chapter 11
Commandment X
PUT IN 100% EFFORT

When you see the winner on the podium, you know it's been a long hard road to get there. Sometimes it can involve luck, but 99% of the time it's when preparation meets opportunity. In that moment, the winners get to claim victory as the best of the best. In Commandment 5, 'The Golden Rule', we explored the commitment to internal responsibility. Even with the best of intentions 'mis-takes' can be made, but leading companies have strategies that provide insurance to reduce 'mis-takes' to a minimum.

One of our clients, who is No.1 and renowned across the world for service excellence (with annual revenue of over half a billion dollars), has been working on this process for generations. Every touchpoint is designed to their best ability and they constantly focus on reducing variation in their first 15% process to a minimum. The first time we delivered their client appreciation results, the owner made a very profound statement. Their results were what many would consider excellent and way above the benchmarks; however, the owner saw an opportunity to raise the bar to new heights and set a totally new set of rules for defining No.1

Their direction was very short but incredibly challenging, 'We have to be **10/10 or nothing**. Anything less and we give our competition an opportunity to take our place'. This commitment paved the way for new KPIs and benchmarks to define their CX process. Their client data is extensive and we deliver information from over 40,000 clients per year. Their CX reporting system turns red when a score for a particular area drops below 9.5/10, and further investigation into the situation is required. Often, it's a touchpoint they don't control, and when these touchpoints are identified, they inform their supplier of the issue and monitor it closely until the score is back in the black.

This is an amazing company that has passed the test of time and all kinds of challenges. They understand they are only as good as their weakest touchpoint.

So, what will it take for you to be this powerful around your CX process?

initiative   empathy
w i l l i n g n e s s
follow up   purpose
o w n e r s h i p

Integrity
110%
Trust

communication
listen   knowledge
u n d e r s t a n d i n g
reliable awareness
e n g a g e m e n t

© Darrell Hardidge. Saguity.com

Chapter 11: Commandment X – PUT IN 100% EFFORT

Consider the following checklist as a strategy that you must have clarity around. 110% commitment is what it takes if you want to be able to dominate your market.

1. Define your WHY and make certain your team are clear and committed to it. Test them by randomly asking people. When they get it correct, praise them; when they don't, have them review it with you to help ensure they understand.

2. Have your CX journey mapped out and very clear to everyone. Your team must understand how everyone is responsible for CX in the company, and that the system is a matrix. Even if it's not their job, it's not OK to ignore a problem. They must take ownership and communicate the issue to the correct person. Remember, *everything speaks.* Every task travels the same road to the tip of the arrow and impacts on CX. This will help your team understand WHY you as a leader do what you do.

Darrell Hardidge

3. The first 15% process is critical for each touchpoint. Anywhere the focus on reducing variation is missing, you risk your CX process being less than optimal. This means you are heading towards the Price Trap. Make sure you test your processes and keep tuning for improvement. Every touchpoint needs a first 15% test. No area can be left out.

4. Master your CX bucket. How is the integrity of your bucket? Do you know or are you guessing for most of it? From our experience, most businesses are guessing until we define what their holes are and WHY. Anywhere you have leaks you are losing money and margin, and it's always in the first 15% of the process. Most importantly, you want to know WHY you have achieved 10/10 for client experiences so you know HOW to replicate them to maximise revenue and profits.

5. Internal responsibility is the hardest of them all because it's all about your leadership and your people. The commitment to being above the line really takes 110% responsibility. We are human and therefore we make 'mis-takes'. It's what we do about it that counts. It's

impossible to seal the leaks in your CX bucket if you have below-the-line behaviour. If it's with a key department or manager, then that touchpoint is now at risk of letting down your CX process.

6. You have to go 'Beyond Expected'. It's not OK to just deliver what your market wants because so will your competitors (at a minimum), and maybe they already are. If this is the case, then you must innovate value, and it must be focused on the heart drivers of appreciation. Going 'Beyond Expected' is hard work and can only be achieved with internal responsibility. However, when you do, the rewards are massive.

7. Clear the fog. Sometimes companies are in the fog and they don't even know it. They just think that it's always like this. You must ensure your team know how to go 'Beyond Expected'. It's impossible to become relevant if you aren't extraordinary. Doing what everyone else does will keep you irrelevant and price driven. Extreme loyalty can only be achieved when you are highly relevant to your

market and the best way to find out is to ask them.

8. Cultivate appreciation. Just think of the people in your life who you appreciate and consider how you feel about them. What would you do for those that you truly appreciate? How far beyond their expectation would you go? When you have reduced the variation in your CX process, you achieve appreciation from your clients. You will be their first and primary thought when it comes to your product or service. They will never be in a fog when trying to remember you. Your relevance is what sits at the front of their mind.

9. Navigate the Price Trap. Many companies are stuck in the Price Trap and don't have any idea why. Just giving what's expected is the false belief that costs companies a fortune and keeps them competing on price. Look around your area and identify highly successful companies that stand out to you. Spend time studying them, and ask the manager/owner if they will give you a few moments to share their WHY with you. Look to what it is that

defines their unique transformational experiences. What is it that separates them from their competition? Understand what things define high levels of value and what it is their market truly appreciates them for.

10. Operate at 110%. The best of the best have an edge. They operate at a level of emotional intelligence that powerfully connects them with their market and guides their innovation. Their secret is **information** and **understanding** of their clients and their needs, both now and in the future. There is no guesswork. There is certainty. If you don't have powerful KPIs that measure your CX process, along with the team's accountability to deliver them, you will never achieve maximum client appreciation.

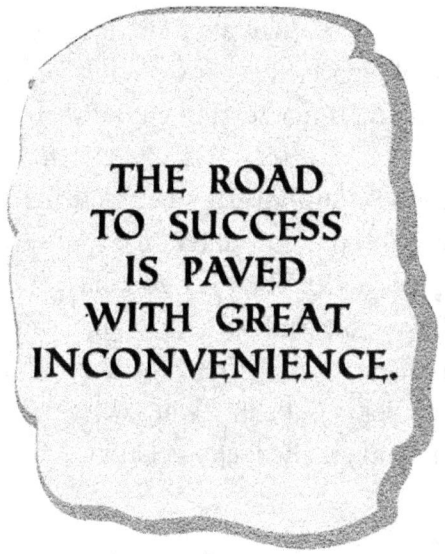

THE ROAD
TO SUCCESS
IS PAVED
WITH GREAT
INCONVENIENCE.

Chapter 11: Commandment X – PUT IN 100% EFFORT

When you are clear on your WHY, and you have your CX journey mapped and refined to the first15% principle, you will understand the integrity of your CX bucket. By operating as a collective committed to the golden rule, you will start to make great headway in your market. When you understand that delivering what's expected is just the start and define your market relevance to stay out of the fog, with a never-ending commitment to reducing variation in your CX process, you will be well underway to the No.1 position.

You can then clearly define your *unique transformational experiences* and have all the ingredients of a No.1 company.

Never lose sight of the goal and never lose your purpose for achieving it. The 10 Commandments are your road map to service excellence and your ability to stake your claim in the marketplace.

Chapter 12
THE TRUTH

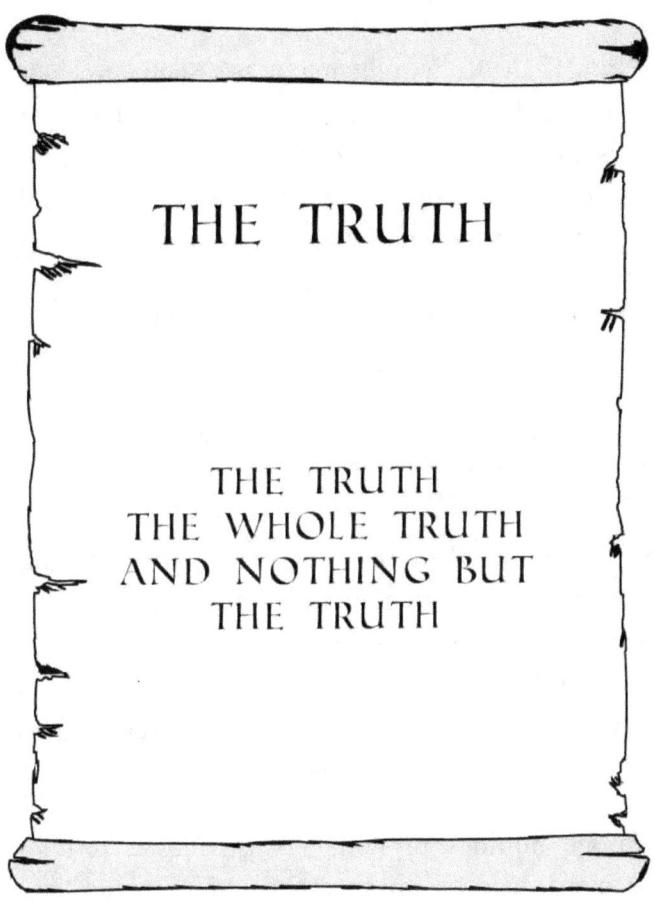

THE TRUTH

THE TRUTH
THE WHOLE TRUTH
AND NOTHING BUT
THE TRUTH

Have you ever observed a court scene in a movie where they have to raise their hand and say, 'I swear to tell the truth, the whole truth and nothing but the truth'?

Getting to the truth of the matter is essential to having clarity and understanding. The most appropriate decisions are made with accurate information, and the evidence and factors are made clear in court. It's the same when making decisions in business.

How do you assess and decide on the most appropriate CX strategy for your company?

Most companies are making vital decisions on CX strategy with little or no information. It's usually based on opinion or gut feel and what may have worked/not worked in the past. If you told most executives their freedom in a court case would be decided using the same principles they use to make decisions in their CX process, most would be horrified. Their concern would be they were going to jail regardless of the proceedings.

We see millions of dollars wasted as a result of decisions made with incorrect information. Every week, I meet with executives who are continuing to pour money down the drain by trying to fill up a leaking CX bucket with resources focused in the wrong area.

The No.1 excuse for a failure to implement a CX strategy is lack of money to invest in the strategy and team training, or being time poor. **They don't have a budget to stop losing money, but they do have a budget to keep wasting it!**

Have a deep think about what your attitude is to investing in a CX strategy?

Chapter 13
ARE YOU A SINNER OR A SAINT

This commandment is not about your personal life and whether or not you are going to heaven or hell. It's about how your business culture and CX process is behaving, and whether it will be a bright or dark future.

In business, there are many forms of leadership and behaviour. Some leaders inspire others to go beyond themselves and achieve greatness, while others spend most of their time trying to motivate people to do the basics. The key point of difference is WHY each person is doing what they are doing. The result will define the way the market experiences the business.

Remember, everyone in your business is responsible for client experience.

Over the last fifteen years, like any director or executive, I've had a lot of meetings. It's interesting that so many of these meetings are also an example of the fog. You remember the great ones, as they usually end up as clients. You also remember some of the not so great, but the bulk are now irrelevant. I observe the intentions and the commitment of how companies behave around their CX process.

Every company you shop with will tell you they really care about you and assure your 'satisfaction'.

Chapter 13: ARE YOU A SINNER OR A SAINT

Why do our life experiences tell us otherwise? Why does our purchasing experience depend on who we purchase from?

Mostly it is due to the values of the company and their leadership. You cannot blame the frontline team, as they were hired and trained by executives who are responsible for their performance. The fact that everyone is responsible for client experience and loyalty means that attitude is always a choice. We all get to choose in every moment how we want to communicate and act.

When I think about my own experiences consulting with executives on their CX process and client loyalty, there are some key distinct differences that stand out. I can almost predict the future decisions with some of them. They all say they really care about their clients and their CX is vital to them; however, their wallet displays a different belief.

Some of my mis-takes have been where I didn't get the 'vibe' of the leadership/company correct. I made the error that every company really cares about its clients, yet the words and actions didn't match. I discovered the fundamental of what truly motivates them: money or achievement.

If the motive is money, then it's usually any quick fix so cash can be made. Often the biggest structural error a company can have is rewarding client acquisition and not having any KPIs on retention. I have had executives say to me that they don't get paid or measured on retention, only on acquisition, so they focus on the quick fix just to get the deal. This is basically saying, 'I'm paid to bring them in the front gate and I don't really care what happens after that, it's not my department or problem'. This is a classic breakdown in the structure of the CX journey. The touchpoints don't connect and the attitude is below-the-line.

If the motive is achievement, then it's a longer-term focus. This is where we experience an above-the-line attitude. They understand that 'Everything Speaks', and achieving great results is a team effort that aims to reduce variation in the CX journey. The focus is on mastering the first 15% of the process and optimising performance and, therefore, profits.

What type of leader are you?

Are you truly committed to mastering your CX process and achieving your highest possible client appreciation index, with maximum profits the reward? Or are you like so many executives who just want a quick fix and a bonus?

If you look into the behaviour of the great leaders, you will see they are always driven by a higher purpose. It's not about them, but rather about the integrity of the team and the company. As Dr Demartini says, 'Until you have a purpose bigger than yourself, you cannot expect to go beyond yourself'. This rings so true when it comes to the purpose and values of a great company. It always shows up in the KPIs of client experience.

The opposite is also true. Look at some of the results of so called great leaders who got the numbers up, got their big bonus, then left the company in a mess for someone else to clean up. There is a highway of carnage littered with badly managed businesses. Their focus was short-term and self-centred.

Your CX process is a true reflection of your commitment to your clients. Most people work hard for their money and, as a bare minimum, they expect who they spend it with to respect them and to stand by what they sold them. So often the business does not consider how much money a client is spending and all their concerns, as it is more focused on its own needs than their clients' needs.

If you have a short-term view and commitment to your clients and are not committed to adopting the 10 Commandments, then you're a sinner. You are not standing by what you say and the marketplace is getting tired of it. Social media has become the modern venue for bagging poorly performing companies with the explosion in exposing poor service.

If you have a true commitment to your clients, and you really want to be known for service excellence and repeat business is your measurement of success, then you're a saint in today's marketplace. The 10 Commandments are designed from tens of thousands of 10/10 client interviews. The best of the best company results have been analysed and the reasons WHY have been the focus.

Review what you are doing now and always place your clients' experience at the centre of everything you do. Remember that everything speaks to your market, and mastering client appreciation is a very challenging task. It will test your resolve beyond what many can imagine; however, the rewards are extreme.

The 10 Commandments of Client Appreciation are your roadmap to staking your claim as a company that's worthy of extreme client loyalty. It's a declaration to your market that you have placed their interests first and are committed to being of service. The No.1 leading companies have their edge, as they are driven by a purpose that is bigger than themselves. It takes a great deal of responsibility to ensure that 'every client experience counts every time'.

To your success in mastering the 10 Commandments of Client Appreciation and earning the right to extreme client loyalty.

Sincerely

Darrell Hardidge

Chapter 14
WHERE TO FROM HERE

There is a certain way that leading companies engage with their markets, and it follows a very strategic approach that ensures every client experience counts — every time.

The 10 Commandments are not just an idea about how to define your service standards, they are very precise principles that, when applied, will produce extraordinary results from your existing client relationships. They will also create the foundations for an extraordinary team culture. They may look simple, but their power and their impact have built amazing companies.

Every week I meet with companies that are seeking to improve their CX process. Unfortunately, many are only committed to the idea of it and end up doing nothing. It's all a bit too hard. They are trapped in the false belief of satisfaction and cannot see their way out. However, there are those who see a bright future and step up to be counted. They are open to the challenges and are prepared to be judged (sometimes harshly) by their market in order to understand their degree of relevance.

Their courage to explore new ways to engage with their market has impacted on the values and culture of their organisation and improved their ability to

Chapter 14: WHERE TO FROM HERE

generate service excellence. This has defined their identity and standards around their CX process. They are also able to produce accurate KPIs that ensure their ability to achieve client appreciation from empowering their teams to be internally responsible and highly accountable.

153

YOU MUST
ACHIEVE THE
STATUS OF
'APPRECIATION
CERTIFIED'.

Chapter 14: WHERE TO FROM HERE

To be awarded with the title 'Appreciation Certified™' is a profound testament to your leadership and to your team's achievement to stand up and be counted. It defines your brand as one that can be trusted. It sends a very powerful statement to your market that declares and defines the culture of your organisation. Only the best achieve this title. It's hard work but it pays and pays, and empowers your team to be the example that excellence is defined by.

To be known as a company that's 'Appreciation Certified™' places you on top of any competitor chasing the myth of satisfaction. Do you want to be aligned with the taxi industry or a service revolutionist like Uber? Avoid client appreciation at your own peril.

If you would like to learn more about the 10 Commandments of Client Appreciation, contact us about delivering the 10 Commandments in-house to your team and we can customise the message to your market. Or contact us for a confidential chat about how to achieve the status of Appreciation Certified™ and design your plan to optimise your CX process.

Our experience and diversity in understanding client appreciation and relevance is what sets us apart. We invented the system and we know how to implement change. If you want to fast track your ability to understand and optimise your market like never before, connect with us and we can design your ideal CX measurement process.

**Always obsess over your clients,
not over your competitors.**

Chapter 15
ABOUT THE AUTHOR

ABOUT
THE
AUTHOR

Darrell Hardidge is an industry-leading expert in optimising client loyalty for businesses and delivers highly effective and engaging team workshops. Known for assisting companies to master their client experience processes; Darrell assists businesses to achieve maximum client loyalty, empowering them to become the market leaders in their fields.

Innovator of the loyalty metric of 'Client Appreciation'; Darrell and his research company Saguity have proven time and again their unique measurement of appreciation solidifies a company's market relevance and separates them from their competitors. Darrell's "Seven step Dy-Val Ladder" encompasses leading business theories into one applicable and proven methodology. These theories are published in his first book '*The Client Revolution*', a successful tool assisting companies to understand how to move beyond 'satisfaction' into the profitable realm of 'appreciation'.

An engaging and leading speaker with the CEO Institute and major corporates; Darrell is highly sought after to deliver in-house seminars and workshops for optimising client experience. His clients vary from CEOs and big business, to academics and entrepreneurs, helping them to design a 10/10 client appreciation culture.

Darrell lives in Melbourne and travels internationally and across Australia working with companies who are truly committed to be the best they can be.